10 Ways To Create Tons Of

Content In Less Time W/O AI

Destiny S. Harris

. . .

. . .

1st Free Gift!

Giving Rocks.

I give away free books daily.

Get your free books today.

Here's how

Step 1: Visit amazon.com/author/destinyharris

Step 2: Filter books by "Price: Low to High"

Step 3: Download available free books

. . .

Table of Contents

. . .

Introduction

Publishers and platforms have questioned how I publish at such high frequencies. **All it takes is effort.** I never had any secrets. I work a lot and have plenty of responsibility, but writing has to remain a constant. The more I publish, the better writer I become, so I stay committed to publishing frequently.

Artificial intelligence is changing the way content is created and the frequency.

Now, authors can have AI write their books for them. But where's the fun in that? Of course, there might be more money in the AI game, but a true writer doesn't only write to get paid; it's their calling.

THEY **WANT** TO WRITE.

But writers still don't always know what to write.

If you still struggle with artist, creator, or writer's block, please know it's not real.

The only block we ever experience is ourselves.

We are frequently our harshest critics.

Worry less about what people think about your writing. Instead, focus on delivering content that your audience or potential new ones would find of value.

Being too self-centered will debilitate artists and prevent them from mastering or practicing their craft.

Create and be consistent.

Worry about perfection later.

The more consistent you are, the more you will flow, which will help you produce more quality content.

There are days when I will bust out 10–20 articles as writing exercises. The goal isn't perfection but to work out my writing muscles.

The faster you can get it done, the harder you work out your writing and thinking muscles, which can help you become a better writer.

. . .

Chapter 1

Write down your ideas throughout the day.

The more you write. The more ideas will come to your mind.

Keep a notepad or a dedicated digital note on your phone or tablet where you can jot down all of your writing ideas.

If you notice something cool, strike up a memorable conversation with someone, learn something new, observe something peculiar, or whatever it is that captures your soul, write it down.

Everything is content. I repeat, everything is content.

. . .

Chapter 2

Write a mixture of long, mid, and short-form articles.

Not everything has to be Harry Potter novel-length.

Not every article has to be a 10-minute read.

Short content can be just as valuable; as long as you focus on eliminating excess and delivering value to your readers, length doesn't matter.

. . .

Chapter 3

Explore multiple topics instead of writing about one thing.

I'm passionate about personal finance, personal development, and health. But these subjects are vast, so there is much to chat about within these areas, which means there are endless subtopics within these primary topics.

Moreover, I also take an interest in writing about writing and social issues.

Whatever intrigues you or you know something about, write about it.

Spread your words to the world. You never know which area your readers will enjoy most.

Experiment. Experiment. Experiment.

. . .

Chapter 4

Write fast, and don't stop typing when you get started.

Someone once told me I must type fast because of all the content I produce.

They weren't wrong. I do type fast, but not as fast as many other writers.

Whenever you start writing, keep going. Force the words to come out until the section or chapter is complete; by performing this exercise, you will exercise and maximize the utilization of your writing muscles.

You're not limited in ideas. You only need to push through to capture the ideas. The more you type and write, the quicker and easier the ideas will come.

. . .

Chapter 5

Attack a previously written article from a different angle.

Challenge yourself by writing an alternate view of a book or article you published.

Not only does this exercise your logical, analytical, and critical thinking skills, but it will help you create more content based on the content you already created.

Instead of starting from scratch, you already have a template, which helps you write faster and easier.

Moreover, you become a better writer. When you can tackle a subject from a different lens, your mind opens.

. . .

Chapter 6

Eliminate distraction. Turn off the phone, and stay off the messaging apps.

Friends and family trying to contact me can sometimes be challenging, and I prefer it that way.

Not only are we an instant-communication-driven society, but we frequently forget that we don't have to respond to people immediately, especially when we have a writing goal in progress.

Put the phone up, turn the TV off (or mute), stay off the internet, and write.

Eliminate yourself from all distractions. If you can't focus in your usual environment, go somewhere you can, so you won't be disturbed.

. . .

Chapter 7

Create outlines for your articles. A few bullets can go a long way and ease the production of a piece.

Got a title but don't know what to write? Well, here are a few questions to get your mind percolating:

1. What thoughts come to mind when you think of the title?

2. What questions come to mind when you think of the title?

3. What experiences come to mind when you think of the title?

4. What questions do you want answered or think others will want answered regarding the title?

Break down titles or even ideas and explore them. Your outline, article, or book will write as itself as you do this.

Approach every idea with some critical thinking skills.

. . .

Chapter 8

Use previously published content as inspiration. So much that we've previously written can be fleshed out more.

When I review articles, posts, or books I publish, I frequently come up with new ideas, angles, or questions to which readers might want answers.

There are also previously published works that need updating or an entire re-write.

You don't need to write new content if you publish a lot and have hundreds or thousands of content artifacts (e.g., articles, books, blog posts, etc.). You already have tons to work with.

. . .

Chapter 9

Don't worry about quality. Just write. Your quality will improve over time. But know that some of your writing will be sh*tty. Some won't. It's okay. There's probably at least one person who will still like it.

There is a lot of garbage I publish. And then there are some things I publish that aren't garbage.

Sometimes, I have limited time and must keep things short and sweet. Sometimes there are errors. Sometimes, the content doesn't even make sense.

Over time, whether you have plenty of time or are in a rush, the quality of your content will improve because practice helps you improve.

Successful authors seem to all agree that **consistently writing** is the most crucial action a writer can ever take.

Practice writing daily. If you don't want to do it daily, practice every other day. But don't just write. Publish. Share your content with the world.

The more you share and publish your work to the public, the more feedback you can get and the sooner you get it.

Don't leave your content in draft mode.

. . .

Chapter 10

Stay consistent. The more you write, the easier it becomes. Moreover, the easier it is for you to enter the flow state.

The previous chapter spoke about consistency, and here we are again on consistency.

If you don't have consistency as a writer, you *can* become successful, but you'll never truly know how successful you could be.

It's easy not to write daily. It's easy not to practice your craft consistently. It's easier to take our passions with a casual approach. But consistency always wins.

The more consistent you are, the closer you will reach your definition of success (whatever success means to you).

Be consistent. Publish daily if possible or close to it.

And if you ever need to take a break from writing, be sure you always come back to it.

. . .

Closing Thoughts

If you're working a full-time job, have a family, and have other obligations, sometimes you can't write 2-8 hours a day to produce the type and amount of content you desire.

Hence, the ability to enter the flow state **quickly** and write incredibly fast is handy.

The more you write, the faster you will write and the better you will write.

Before we end the book, here are a few ergonomic tips for writers, content creators, or people frequently on their computers or devices.

Ergo Body Tips For Your Writing Sessions

- Take standing breaks when writing for
  long periods so your muscles don't tense.

- Look up or straight ahead. Avoid looking
  down. Your body should feel comfortable
  100% of the time and mimic your natural
  positioning.

- Take walks throughout your writing
  sessions; this will increase your
  inspiration, release endorphins, and
  ensure your muscles don't become too
  tense. When you go for walks, try to

avoid looking at screens. Look at things

outside far away to rest your eyes.

. . .

Thank You For Reading

Thank you for reading this book.

Stay blessed, lucky, favored, aware, joyous, and committed to bettering yourself.

. . .

The End.

. . .

About Destiny S. Harris

Destiny S. Harris' goal is to positively inspire, cultivate, elevate, and educate the minds of individuals across the globe through her writing.

Creating (whether books, courses, articles, poetry, or music) has always been Destiny's thing, not to mention health & fitness and all things entrepreneurial. Destiny published her first book, "Beauty Secrets for Girls," at age 11 and her second book, "Don't Wait Until It's Too Late," at age 12.

Destiny obtained three degrees in Psychology, Political Science, & Cultural Studies. She also started her own music teaching business at the age of 14, which she led for over ten years. In addition, she has been teaching academic, career, and personal development topics to thousands of students and readers since 2004.

Outside of writing, Destiny loves and enjoys a few other things: reading, weightlifting, traveling, football, dogs, food, classic movies, mountain and ocean views, sleeping, plants, and nature.

Check out her work, leave a review, share your thoughts with your friends and family, and be a part of a movement: helping people learn and grow through means of self-education (books).

Complete the Steps To Get Free eBooks:

Step 1: Go to amazon.com/author/destinyharris

Step 2: Filter books by "Price: Low to High"

Step 3: Download available free books

. . .

Connect W/ Destiny S. Harris

Please reach out and stay in touch. Destiny S. Harris enjoys chatting with readers.

Start a conversation today @ destinyh.com

. . .

Free Gifts!

Access courses & free eBooks at the link below:

destinyh.com

. . .